Uniquely Indiana

D.J. Ross

Heinemann Library
Chicago, Illinois

Designed by Heinemann Library
Printed and bound in the United States by
Lake Book Manufacturing, Inc.

07 06 05 04 03
10 9 8 7 6 5 4 3 2 1

**Library of Congress
Cataloging-in-Publication Data**

Ross, D. J.
   Uniquely Indiana / D. J. Ross.
        p. cm.—(Heinemann state studies)
Summary: Examines what makes Indiana unique,
including its history, geography, people, culture,
and attractions.
Includes bibliographical references and index.
   ISBN 1-4034-4490-0 (HC library binding) --
ISBN 1-4034-4505-2 (PB)
   1. Indiana—Juvenile literature. [1. Indiana.]
I. Title. II. Series.
   F526.3.R67 2003
   977.2—dc21

                                   2003009432

Acknowledgments
Development and photo research by
BOOK BUILDERS LLC

The author and publishers are grateful to the following for permission to reproduce copyright
material:

Cover photographs by (top, L-R) Paul Riley, Indiana
University Athletics; Layne Kennedy/Corbis; Joseph
Sohm, ChromoSohm Inc./Corbis; Richard
Cummins/Corbis; (main) Ron McQueeney/Artemis
Images

Title page (L-R) Mark Gibson/Midwestock; Paul Riley,
Indiana University Athletics; AP/Wide World Photos;
9, 41, 45 International Mapping Associates; pp. 4,
14BR, 16, 40 Daniel Dempster/Bruce Coleman Inc.;
p. 5 Richard Cummins/Corbis; pp. 6, 45 Layne
Kennedy/Corbis; p. 8 James P. Rowan; p. 10 Courtesy
of Delphi-Delco Electronic Systems; p. 11 Mary Ann
Boysen; p. 12T Joseph Sohm, ChromoSohm Inc./
Corbis; p. 13L Bonnie Sue/Photo Researchers, Inc.; p.
13R Leonard Lee Rue/Photo Researchers, Inc.; p.
14TL Stephen J. Krasemann/Photo Researchers, Inc.;
p. 17, 20L, 20BR Culver Pictures; p. 18 Medford
Historical Society Collection/Corbis; p. 20 TR Courtesy of ConverseRubber Co.; p. 21T Courtesy Office
Congresswoman Julia Carson; p. 21B Courtesy Indi-
ana State University Archives; p. 22 Ron McQueeney/
Artemis Images; p. 23 AFP/Corbis; p. 25T Bettmann/
Corbis; p. 25B Mark Gibson/Midwestock; p. 26
Courtesy Supreme Court Indiana; p. 28 Richmond Art
Museum, Indiana; p. 29 Elkhart County Convention
and Visitors Bureau; p. 30 Laurie Vogt/StockFood;
pp. 31, 43B Courtesy New York Public Library; p. 32
Indiana State Museum/Karen Carr; p. 34 Paul Riley,
Indiana University Athletics; p. 35 Bettmann/Corbis;
p. 36 AP/Wide World Photos; p. 37 Courtesy
Valparaiso Community Festivals and Events; p. 38
Courtesy Ball State University; p. 39 Gene Ahren/
Bruce Coleman Inc.; p. 43T Courtesy Indiana State
Fair; p. 44 Vandystat/Photo Researchers, Inc.; p. 45
Jim Steinhart/www.PlanetWare.com.

Special thanks to Wilma L. Gibbs of the Indiana
Historical Society for her expert comments in the
preparation of this book.

Every effort has been made to contact copyright
holders of any material reproduced in this book.
Any omissions will be rectified in subsequent
printings if notice is given to the publisher.

Some words are shown in bold, **like this.**
You can find out what they mean by looking
in the glossary.

Contents

Uniquely Indiana

Sweeping sand dunes, fertile farmland, thick forests, modern industry, and broad rivers make Indiana a unique, one-of-a-kind state. Located in the midwestern United States, Indiana is bordered by Michigan, Ohio, Kentucky, and Illinois, as well as Lake Michigan. The name *Indiana* means "Land of the Indians." But the more than six million people who live in Indiana call themselves *Hoosiers*.

WHAT IS A HOOSIER?

No one knows for sure where the name *Hoosier* came from, although there are many ideas. One of the most common explanations stems from pioneer days in the 1800s, when people would often answer a knock at the door with "Who's here?" Perhaps they said it so fast it sounded similar to "Hoosier." It may also come from the word *hushers*, a term once used for Indiana rivermen, who were always ready for a fight. They were called "hushers" because they usually won, "hushing" their foes. Over time, perhaps "hushers" became "Hoosiers." Hoosier has been in everyday use since the 1830s.

Some popular destinations in the Indiana Dunes include the Gaylord Butterfly Preserve, Heron Rookery, Pinhook Bog, and the Calumet, Hobart, and Hoosier Prairies.

MAJOR CITIES

Indianapolis is the capital of Indiana and its largest city with a population of more than 800,000. Indiana's lawmakers chose the site of Indianapolis because it is near the center of the state and about 75 miles from half of the farms in Indiana. Today, the city is often called the "Crossroads of America" because more interstate highways cross the city than any other in the country. Indianapolis was modeled after Washington, D.C., the nation's capital. In 1821 Indianapolis was laid out on a mile-square grid with Monument Circle in the center.

Indianapolis is the largest U.S. city that is not on a major river.

Today, Monument Circle is home to the Soldiers and Sailors Monument. The monument, commemorating the **Civil War** (1861–1865), was the first in the nation dedicated to the ordinary soldier rather than a well-known hero. Completed in 1901, the squared limestone **obelisk** juts 284 feet, 6 inches into the air.

Fort Wayne, located in northeastern Indiana, is the second largest city in the state. The area was once home to the Miami Native Americans. In the 1600s and 1700s, the French and British canoed down the St. Mary's, St. Joseph, and Maumee rivers, which meet at Fort Wayne, as they explored the region. Later, in 1794, General "Mad" Anthony Wayne defeated the Miami Native Americans and built the first U.S. fort at the site. People began moving into the fort on October 21, 1794. The next day it was officially named "Fort Wayne," and October 22 is celebrated as the city's birthday. The National Basketball Association (NBA) was born in Fort Wayne in 1946.

Completed around 1890, the Old Vanderburgh County Courthouse is built of Indiana limestone.

Far to the south on the Ohio River sits Evansville, the third largest city in the state. Founded in 1812, Evansville was named after Robert M. Evans, an early local leader. It quickly grew, and in the 1840s thousands of German immigrants came to the area looking for new farmland. Evansville is home to the Willard Library, which opened its doors in 1885. More than 115 years old, Willard is one of the oldest public libraries in the midwest. Willard Carpenter donated the money for the building, noting that it was to be "a public library for the use of the people of all classes, races, and sexes, free of charge forever."

Gary's Steel Industry

In the early 1900s Elbert H. Gary, the president of the U.S. Steel Company, planned a new city in northwestern Indiana on the shore of Lake Michigan—close to Chicago and to railroad transportation. He called his city Gary and designed it to be a model company town for the workers who would eventually operate a new, state-of-the-art steel mill, Gary Works.

Gary Works opened in 1908 and quickly grew. Soon, the mill produced raw steel, rails, wire, rods, pipes, tubes, and wheels. Gary Works rapidly became U.S. Steel's leading steel mill. By 1930 Gary Works became known as "one of the industrial wonders of the 1900s." Today, Gary remains a leading steel center as automation of the mills increased production.

Indiana's Geography and Climate

Indiana is relatively flat in the north but hilly in the south. Fertile farmland and a **temperate climate** help make Indiana a leading farm state.

INDIANA'S LAND

Geographers divide Indiana into three main regions—the Great Lakes Plains, the Tipton Till Plains, and the Southern Hill Country.

The Great Lakes Plains cover the northern third of the state. Near Lake Michigan are large sand dunes, and farther inland are swamps and marshes. This part of Indiana is a major industrial center known for steel mills and factories because of the nearby transportation offered by Lake Michigan and the rail lines of Chicago.

The rich soil of the Tipton Till Plain covers the center of the state. Here farmers grow corn, soybeans, and other

Making Indiana's Lakes

About 14,000 years ago glaciers helped form Indiana's lakes. In northern Indiana, evidence of glaciers include **moraines** and marshes and swamps. Because of the glaciers, most of Indiana's natural lakes are found in the northern third of the state.

The Wabash River flows through Indiana and forms part of the state's border with Illinois.

grains. They also raise hogs and dairy cattle. Hoosier Hill, the highest point in the state at 1,257 feet above sea level, is in the eastern part of this region.

The Southern Hill Country makes up part of southern Indiana. It is the region where the Wabash River flows into the Ohio River. The Wabash carries particles of rich soil, called **silt,** from the Tipton Till Plain. The Southern Hill Country also holds rich deposits of coal. During the Ice Age, about 14,000 years ago, **glaciers** covered about 80 percent of present-day Indiana. The glaciers wore down the land, leaving the northern parts of the state flat. A section of Southern Hill Country, called the Driftless Area, is the only part of Indiana not covered by glaciers.

INDIANA'S CLIMATE

Because of its location inland, Indiana has a **humid-continental climate.** There are no oceans nearby to cool Indiana in the summer or warm it in the winter. Lake Michigan, however, moderates the temperature in the northwestern part of the state. This happens because the water in Lake Michigan cools more slowly than the nearby land. As a result, the shore stays cooler than land that is farther away from the lake.

In winter, cold arctic winds swoop down from Canada, bringing freezing temperatures and snow. The state has no large hills or mountains to block the winds. As the winds cross Lake Michigan, they pick up moisture, thus increasing the snowfall in northern Indiana. The large snowfall is called lake-effect snow.

Evansville

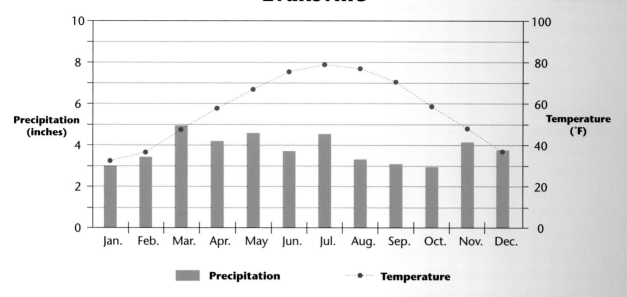

Precipitation (inches) · Temperature (°F)

Precipitation · Temperature

Indianapolis

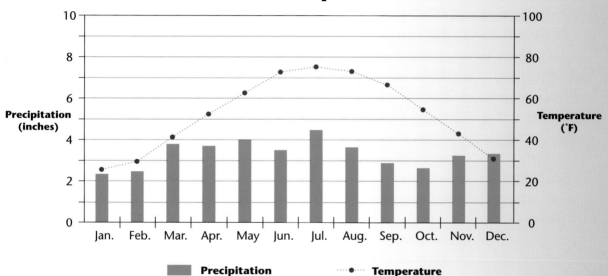

Precipitation (inches) · Temperature (°F)

Precipitation · Temperature

Evansville, located in southern Indiana, has warmer summer temperatures than does Indianapolis, found in the central part of the state.

In summer, winds from the Gulf of Mexico blow north and bring moist, warm air to Indiana, helping to create humid summers. When these warm winds meet cooler winds from the north, thunderstorms, sometimes accompanied by violent windstorms called **tornadoes,** threaten Indiana. Indianapolis, located in the center of the state, receives about 40 inches of precipitation each year.

Famous Firsts

AUTOMOTIVE FIRSTS

In 1893 Kokomo resident Elwood Haynes became a pioneer in the auto industry. He purchased a gasoline-powered engine and designed one of the first "horseless carriages," making the trial run in 1894. Haynes then went on to invent the muffler to keep his new automobile quiet. Haynes also experimented with metals and invented many different **alloys.** Among them was stainless steel. He also developed an alloy used in the exploration of space.

The Duesenberg Motor Company built its first car in Indianapolis in 1920. Called a Model A, it included many innovations such as an eight-cylinder engine and safer brakes.

In 1947 Delco invented the first signal-seeking car radio, where the radio automatically finds the best signal. This invention provided clearer sound and less static. In 1957 Delco made the first all-**transistor** car radio. Before that time, car radios included fragile glass tubes that had to warm up before the radio could play, a process that took several minutes.

Kokomo's Delco Radio Company created the first push-button car radio for General Motors in 1938.

TECHNOLOGY FIRSTS

Dr. Richard Gatling patented the first rapid-fire gun in Indianapolis in 1862. Known as the Gatling Gun, it is a hand-driven, crank-operated, multi-barreled machine gun able to shoot 200 rounds per minute. Invented during the **Civil War** (1861–1865), Gatling believed his invention would end war by making it unthinkable to use such a horrible weapon.

Workers in Columbus, Indiana, built the first **diesel-**powered tractor in 1930.

In 1928 Kemp Brothers Canning Company made the first canned tomato juice. The company in Kokomo developed the product at the request of a doctor who was searching for new baby foods to use in his clinic.

ENTERTAINMENT FIRSTS

Johnny Gruelle of Indianapolis designed and patented the Raggedy Ann doll in 1915. Gruelle was a cartoonist whose early drawings were for adults. Later, he started drawing for children. In 1922 his comic strip, "The Adventures of Raggedy Ann and Andy," appeared in newspapers across the country. By the time of his death in 1938, Gruelle's characters were famous around the world.

The first Raggedy Ann doll belonged to Johnny Gruelle's daughter, Marcella.

The Regency Division of Industrial Development Engineering Associates (I.D.E.A.) manufactured the world's first transistor radio, the Regency TR-1, in Indianapolis in 1954. "See it! Hear it! Get it!" read the ads. It was truly the world's first pocket-sized radio—3 inches by 5 inches by 1.25 inches—and weighed 12 ounces. Powered by a small battery, it came in only four colors—black, gray, maroon, and ivory. About 100,000 radios sold for $49.95 each the first year! With the transistor radio, listeners could take music, news, and sports with them.

Indiana's State Symbols

INDIANA STATE FLAG

Indiana artist Paul Hadley designed the present state flag in 1916, winning a contest celebrating the state's **centennial.** Indiana lawmakers officially adopted the flag the following year.

The flaming torch stands for liberty and **enlightenment.** Six "rays of light" coming from that torch symbolize these two ideas. The thirteen stars that form the outer circle represent the original thirteen states in the United States. The five stars that make up the inner circle represent the next five states admitted to the Union. The largest star, located below the state name, represents Indiana, the nineteenth state.

INDIANA STATE SEAL

The Indiana state seal has been used since the 1800s, but was not officially adopted until 1963.

STATE MOTTO: THE CROSSROADS OF AMERICA

Indiana's motto, The Crossroads of America, was adopted in 1937. The original state crossroads were rivers, the **National Road,** and the railways. Today, the name refers to the interstate highways that crisscross the state, such as I-70, I-69, and I-65.

STATE SONG: "ON THE BANKS OF THE WABASH, FAR AWAY"

"On the Banks of the Wabash, Far Away" by Paul Dresser became the Indiana state song in 1913.

STATE FLOWER: PEONY

White, pink, or deep red peonies flower in Indiana gardens in late May and early June. The state representative who proposed making the peony the state flower was a commercial peony grower.

"On the Wabash,

'Round my India
   cornfields,
In the distance l
   and cool.
Oftentimes my t
   childhood,
Where I first rece
   school.
But one thing th
   picture,
Without her face
I long to see my
As she stood the
   greet.

CHORUS

Oh, the moonlight's fair tonight along the
   Wabash,
From the fields there comes the breath of
   new mown hay.
Through the sycamores the candle lights
   are gleaming,
On the banks of the Wabash, far away.

STATE TREE: TULIP TREE

In 1931, the state assembly adopted the tulip tree, also known as the yellow poplar, as the state tree because it once was the most familiar tree in Indiana's forests.

Many people use the tulip tree in ornamental gardens.

STATE BIRD: CARDINAL

The cardinal became the state bird in 1933. Cardinals are one of the few species of birds that stay in Indiana during the winter.

INDIANA STATE QUARTER

Hoosiers got their first official look at the Indiana state quarter on August 8, 2002, at the Indianapolis Motor Speedway. The quarter shows an Indy car, celebrating the world-famous Indianapolis 500 and the Indianapolis Motor Speedway.

The car races over the state outline and past a circle of nineteen stars, recalling that Indiana was the nineteenth state to join the Union.

STATE STONE: SALEM LIMESTONE

Adopted as the state stone in 1971 Salem limestone is quar
tral and southern Indiar
have used it in the Ind
across the country, inclu
New York City and the

Salem limestone is known for its attractive color, strength, and toughness.

Indiana's History and People

Native Americans lived in what is today Indiana for thousands of years before Europeans arrived in the 1600s.

EARLY CULTURES

Most of the Native Americans living in what is today Indiana belonged to the Miami nation. We know about these early people through the **artifacts,** such as pottery and tools, they left behind. The Miami were a part of the Algonquians, which also included the Delaware, Potawatomi, Kickapoo, and Shawnee. But the Miami were the largest group of Algonquians.

The First Europeans in Indiana

The first Europeans may have come to what is today Indiana as early as 1541. Hernando de Soto, a Spanish explorer, is said to have crossed the Ohio River to Aquixo, a Native American settlement. This settlement was located in the area now known as Angel Mounds State Park. He then traveled to the town of Casqui, thought to be Vincennes.

Samuel de Champlain, the governor of **New France,** might have visited the Maumee (Miami) in northern Indiana in about 1614. French explorers Robert de LaSalle and Louis Joliet traveled in the area in the mid-1600s and claimed the land for France.

The Miami lived in villages. Each spring the men would help the women clear the fields for planting. The women were then responsible for planting and harvesting the crops—usually corn, pumpkins, beets, and squash. After the harvest, the entire village celebrated with a large festival. In the fall, the men left the villages to hunt for deer, rabbits, bears, and beavers. These animals provided meat, and their skins and fur were made into clothing.

In the 1600s the French traders who arrived in what is today Indiana met the Lenape, Native Americans who lived in the Ohio River Valley. They were **nomadic,** following the animals they hunted. They traded furs and other goods with the French. While the French focused on trade, British settlers set up thirteen colonies along the Atlantic coast of North America.

The George Rogers Clark Memorial stands where historians believe Fort Sackville once stood. The inscription above the sixteen columns reads, "The Conquest of the West—George Rogers Clark and The Frontiersmen of the American Revolution."

THE AMERICAN REVOLUTION

In the 1760s and 1770s, the British and the colonists disagreed over how the thirteen colonies should be governed. They also argued over taxes. As a result, the American Revolution broke out between Great Britain and the American colonists in 1775.

When the American Revolution began, the British held many forts in the Ohio River Valley, including Fort Sackville, near present-day Vincennes, Indiana. From these forts, the British sent Native American warriors to attack American settlers. George Rogers Clark, an American colonel, organized a militia to defend the settlers from

The Battle of Tippecanoe

The Battle of Tippecanoe stands as the most famous fight in Indiana. Tecumseh, a Shawnee chief, and his brother, known as the Prophet, tried to unite Native Americans with the aim of protecting their lands. In November 1811, William Henry Harrison, governor of the Indiana Territory, gathered a huge force of American troops. They marched toward the Native Americans' settlement at Prophetstown, on the Tippecanoe River. The Prophet attacked first, and a bloody battle followed. Crushed, Tecumseh and his supporters fled north to Canada.

these attacks. Clark and about 170 American and French troops surrounded the fort and forced the British to surrender it on February 25, 1779, thus ending the Battle of Vincennes.

The Americans held the Ohio River Valley for the rest of the war. Because of Clark's bravery, the British **ceded** the area to the new United States at the war's end. This vast region, later called the Northwest Territory, makes up the present-day states of Ohio, Indiana, Illinois, Michigan, Wisconsin, and northeastern Minnesota.

THE NORTHWEST ORDINANCE

After the American Revolution, few settlers lived in what is today Indiana. Congress passed the Northwest Ordinance in 1787 to govern this almost empty land. This law did three important things. First, it gave the settlers many rights, including freedom of religion, property rights, and trial by jury. Second, the law made slavery illegal in the Northwest Territory. Finally, the law set up how the new states formed from the territory could join the Union.

Tecumseh died in 1813.

STATEHOOD

By early 1815 the population of the Indiana Territory had grown to more than 63,000 people. Congress then passed a law that permitted the people to elect **delegates** to write a state constitution. This 1816 document became the basis for the new state's first government.

The new constitution included three sections that were unique to Indiana. One section allowed Indiana's people to vote if they wanted a new constitution. Another called for a state-supported education system—from elementary schools to college. The third section outlawed private banks because, in other states, they often closed, taking people's money.

The law admitting Indiana "into the Union on an equal footing with the original states, in all respects whatever" was signed by President James Madison on December 11, 1816. This day is celebrated as Indiana's birthday.

INDIANA IN THE CIVIL WAR

Indiana was one of the first states to respond to President Abraham Lincoln's call for volunteers to put down the rebellion that became known as the **Civil War** (1861–1865). At first, more Hoosiers volunteered than the government thought were needed. Like other states, Indiana raised millions of dollars to equip and feed its soldiers.

Until 1863, only white Americans could join the military. That year, Governor Oliver Perry Morton allowed Indiana's African Americans to volunteer. They fought in a separate regiment, the 28th U.S. Colored

More than 208,000 Hoosiers served in the Union armies during the Civil War.

Regiment. African Americans came from all over the state to enlist. A few even came from Kentucky. These soldiers guarded Washington, D.C., and then led the Union attack on Petersburg, Virginia, in 1865.

AFTER THE CIVIL WAR

After the Civil War ended in 1865, Indiana grew rapidly. Its farms became more productive. Industry developed, especially in the northern part of the state. A network of railroads transformed such cities as Indianapolis, Evansville, and South Bend into important centers of trade.

During the 1950s Indiana's economy continued to become more industrial. New farm equipment replaced many workers, who left the farms to find jobs in the city. To meet the state's growing energy needs, Clifty Creek, one the nation's largest power plants, was built on the Ohio River west of Madison in 1956.

In the late 1900s and early 2000s, Indiana's economy grew more service based. That is, more and more workers were employed in banks, insurance companies, transportation, and communications industries, rather than in producing goods such as steel or cars.

FAMOUS PEOPLE FROM INDIANA

Benjamin Harrison (1833–1901), politician. The only president elected from Indiana, Harrison served in several state offices and then became a U.S. senator in 1880. In 1888, Harrison, a **Republican,** won the presidency in a close election. President Harrison signed the Sherman Anti-trust bill, a law that protects trade and commerce.

James Whitcomb Riley (1849–1916), poet. Known as the "Hoosier Poet," Riley hailed from Greenfield. He wrote many of his poems in colorful local language, called Hoosier dialect. Two of his most famous children's poems are "Little Orphan Annie" and "The Runaway Boy."

Charles "Chuck" Taylor (1901–1969), businessleader. After playing basketball for the Akron Firestones, Taylor became a salesman for the Converse shoe company in 1921. He promoted their "All-Star" basketball shoe as well the game itself. Because he improved the sneaker's design and was so successful in promoting it, the company added Taylor's name to the "All-Star" shoes' ankle patch in 1923. Converse sold more than 500 million pairs of "Chucks."

Taylor was born in Brown County, Indiana.

A 1955 auto accident cut short Dean's promising movie career.

James Dean (1931–1955), actor. Born in Marion and reared in Fairmont, Indiana, Dean made only three movies in his short acting career—*East of Eden, Giant,* and *Rebel Without a Cause.* Dean is still remembered by fans for his roles as a troubled youth of the 1950s.

Grissom graduated from Purdue University in 1950.

Virgil "Gus" Grissom (1926–1967), astronaut. Born in Mitchell, Indiana, Grissom became one of the first seven astronauts in 1959. In 1961 he made the second successful **suborbital** flight in the *Liberty Bell 7.* In 1967 Grissom and two other astronauts died when a fire swept through the *Apollo 1* command module during a launch pad test.

Kurt Vonnegut (1922–), writer. Born and reared in Indianapolis, Vonnegut is famous for his novels that combine science fiction and humor, including *Slaughterhouse Five* (1969) and *Timequake* (1997).

Julia Carson (1938–), politician. Carson was born in Louisville, Kentucky, but grew up in Indianapolis, where she began her political career. Voters elected her to the U.S. House of Representatives in 1996. She became the first woman and the first African American to represent Indianapolis in Congress.

Voters re-elected Julia Carson to Congress in 2002.

Twyla Tharp (1942–), dancer and choreographer. Tharp was born in Portland, Indiana. The more than 90 dances she created combine elements of ballet, jazz, modern dance, and tap. She is famous for arranging the dances in the movies *Hair, Amadeus,* and *Ragtime.*

David Letterman (1947–), entertainer. Letterman grew up in Indianapolis and attended Ball State University. He worked as a newsman and weather forecaster before moving to Los Angeles in 1975. There, he launched his career as a comedian. He appeared on the *The Tonight Show* several times and currently stars in his own late-night television show.

Larry Bird led Indiana State to the NCAA title game in 1979.

Larry Bird (1956–), athlete and coach. Bird, of French Lick, Indiana, gained fame as a basketball superstar. A star player at Indiana State, he holds 30 Indiana state records, including most points (2,850), steals (240), and rebounds (1,247). He began his pro career with the Boston Celtics in 1979 and went on to win three NBA championships.

The Indy 500

The world's top racecar drivers have been coming to Indianapolis to show off their skills at "The Greatest Spectacle in Racing" since 1911! Today, the annual Indy 500 attracts more than 250,000 fans from around the world.

The Early Years

Carl Fisher, an early automobile dealer, started the Indianapolis Motor Speedway in 1909 as a testing ground for new cars—many of which were made in Indiana. The track, a 2-mile rectangle, was made of 3.2 million bricks. During the first race in August 1909, disaster struck as the track's surface broke up and six people died.

The first 500-mile classic, called the International Sweepstakes, ran on May 30, 1911. The winner, Ray Harroun of Pennsylvania, raced at an average speed of 74.59 miles per hour. At the 1919 race, Howdy Wilcox became the first driver to break 100 miles per hour.

The tough racecourse varies in width from 50 feet on the straight stretches to 60 feet on the turns.

In 1945, Tony Hulman, a business leader, bought the racetrack for $750,000. To get the track ready for the May 1946 race, Hulman spent millions of dollars, resulting in a greatly improved raceway, making it safer and providing better viewing for the fans. Since then, other advances upgraded the Speedway, including an eight-story control tower.

THE RACE TODAY

Today, most of the original 3.2 million bricks are paved with asphalt—except for a 36-inch stretch that designates the start/finish line.

The speedway permitted women to race in 1971. Janet Guthrie became the first woman to qualify for the race in 1977. Willie T. Ribbs became the first African American to qualify for the race in 1991. In 2001, Cory Witherill, a Navajo, became the first Native American to race in the Indy 500.

Arie Luyendyk won the Indy 500 in 1990 and again in 1997. His son, Arie Jr., also races Indy cars.

Arie Luyendyk, from the Netherlands, set the race record of 185.981 miles per hour for the full 500 miles in 1990—over 100 miles per hour faster than the 1911 winner! After cruising into Victory Lane, the winner is handed a bottle of milk, the traditional drink of Indy's champion. Milk became the drink of champions after the 1936 winner, Louis Meyer, was photographed gulping down a bottle of buttermilk, his favorite drink.

The Hall of Fame Museum

Founded in 1952, the Hall of Fame Museum is located on the grounds of the Indianapolis Motor Speedway. The museum honors outstanding racers as well as the automobile industry. A new building, which opened in 1976, houses about 75 classic racecars. Several antique passenger cars are also on display. Many of the cars, such as Stutz, Cole, Marmon, National, and Duesenberg, were built in Indianapolis. The museum was designated a National Historic Landmark in 1987.

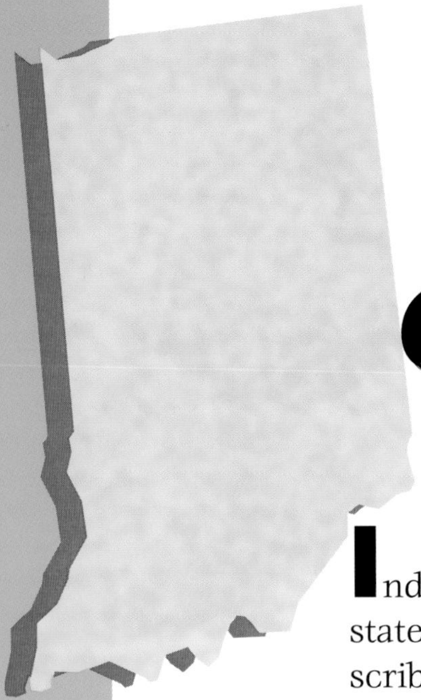

Indiana's State Government

Indiana's government is based in Indianapolis, the state's capital. A constitution, or plan of government, describes how the state is to be governed.

The constitution that governs Indiana today went into effect in 1851. It promises many freedoms for Hoosiers—including freedom of religion, speech, and the press. These rights are

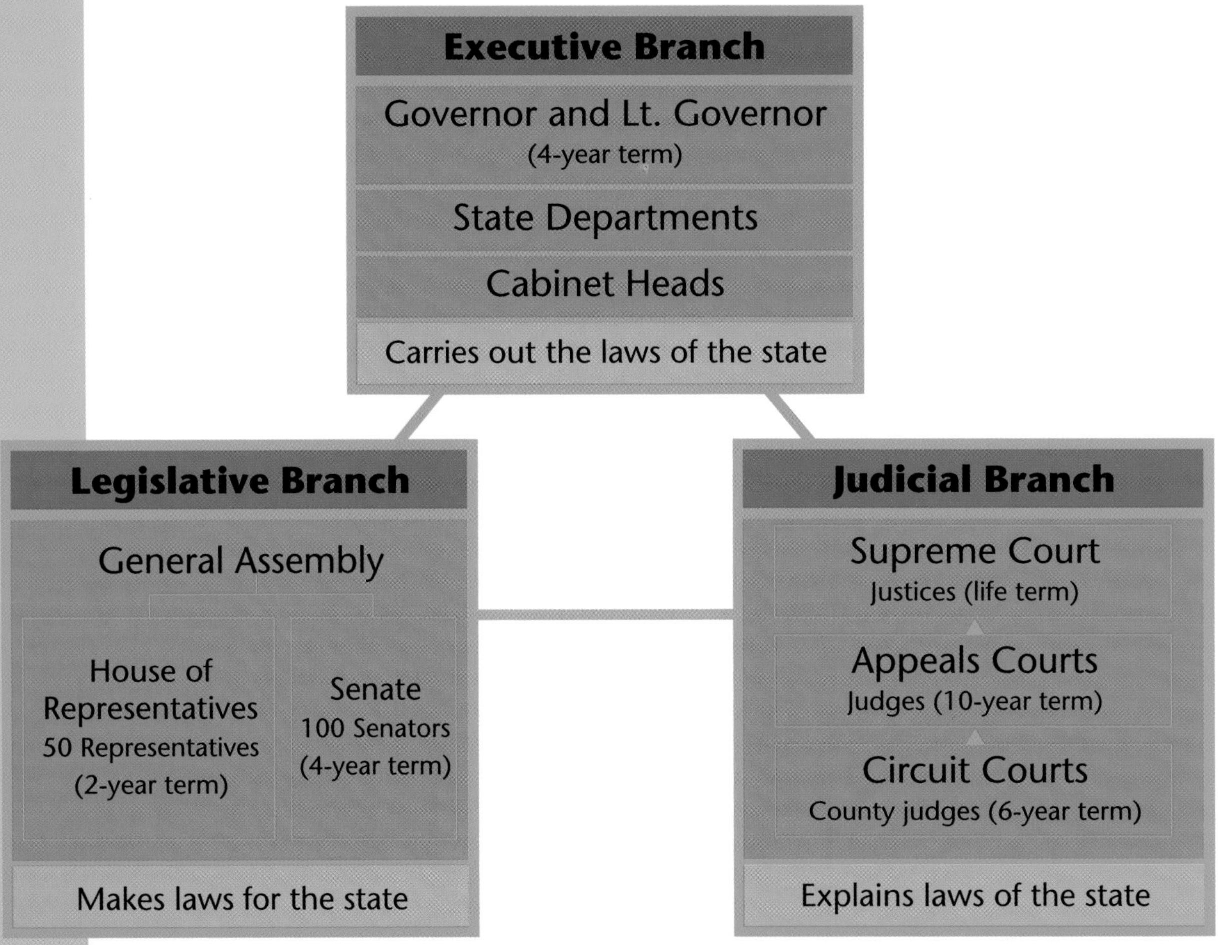

Executive Branch

Governor and Lt. Governor
(4-year term)

State Departments

Cabinet Heads

Carries out the laws of the state

Legislative Branch

General Assembly

House of Representatives
50 Representatives
(2-year term)

Senate
100 Senators
(4-year term)

Makes laws for the state

Judicial Branch

Supreme Court
Justices (life term)

Appeals Courts
Judges (10-year term)

Circuit Courts
County judges (6-year term)

Explains laws of the state

based on those guaranteed in the U.S. Constitution.

Indiana's government is similar to the **federal government** in Washington, D.C. It too is made up of three branches—the legislative, the executive, and the judicial.

Legislators meet in the state capitol and make the laws that the executive branch enforces.

LEGISLATIVE BRANCH

The legislative branch, called the Indiana General Assembly, makes the state's laws. It consists of two houses—the senate and the house of representatives. The senate's 50 members are elected to four-year terms. The house's 100 members are elected to two-year terms.

Work on the Capitol began in 1880 and finished in 1888. A 1988 restoration returned the building to its original appearance.

A bill, or proposed law, may start in either house of the General Assembly, except for bills about taxes. These bills must start in the house of representatives. A bill must be approved by more than half of the members of both houses before it can be sent to the governor. If the governor signs the bill, it becomes a law. If the governor vetoes, or rejects, the bill, it does not become a law.

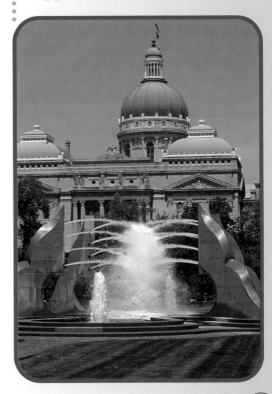

EXECUTIVE BRANCH

The executive branch carries out the laws and runs the state from day to day. The governor is the head of this branch. The lieutenant governor is the second-highest state official. Voters elect these leaders to a four-year term of office. Voters elect other executive branch officials as well. For example, the secretary of state oversees elections and helps regulate business, and the treasurer collects the tax money that is due to Indiana.

JUDICIAL BRANCH

The judicial branch interprets Indiana's laws. Indiana has three levels of state courts—the circuit courts, the appellate court, and the supreme court.

The circuit courts, organized at the county level, hear civil and criminal cases. Civil cases center on disagreements between people or companies. Criminal cases involve a charge of breaking a law. Voters elect circuit court judges, who serve six-year terms.

The **appellate court** only hears **appeals cases.** In the appellate courts, a panel of three judges hears each case and reaches a decision. There is no **jury.** The governor appoints appellate judges for a term of two years. Then the voters may elect the judges for ten-year terms. Appellate judges may serve on the court for life. A special appellate court with one judge is the tax court. This court hears cases concerning the state's tax laws.

The Indiana Supreme Court is the highest court in the state. It has the final say in legal matters. The chief justice heads the court and is responsible for the court system. Like the appellate court, the Indiana Supreme Court mostly hears appeals. Supreme court justices are appointed by the governor and may serve for life.

The Indiana Supreme Court heads the state's judicial branch.

Indiana's Culture

Hoosiers have deep cultural roots that reflect the many people who live in the state. Although Indiana is still a leading farm state, over the years it has contributed notably to the nation's culture.

A RURAL HERITAGE

In the early 1800s, Indiana's rich soil and good climate attracted settlers from eastern and southern states. These early settlers brought their farming heritage with them.

Beginning around 1830, more people from Europe moved to Indiana. English, Irish, French, German, Norwegian, Polish, and Italian immigrants were among those who came to call Indiana home. Some of these groups continued to farm, but others took jobs building canals and, later, railroads. Although new immigrants from Latin America and Asia continue to bring their culture to Indiana, about 97 percent of the state's people are born in the state.

INDIANA WRITERS, ARTISTS, AND CRAFTERS

Indiana has given the nation and the world many cultural gifts. Photography, literature, art, and sculpture are all part of Indiana's cultural landscape.

In the late 1880s, Gene Stratton Porter (1863–1924) took striking photographs of birds and animals in their natural habitat. She wrote articles for an early photography magazine. She later wrote novels about her life in Indiana. Among her most famous works are *A Girl of the Limberlost, Laddie, Michael O'Halloran,* and *A Daughter of the Land.*

T. C. Steele, perhaps the most famous artist of the Hoosier Group, painted In the Whitewater Valley *in 1899.*

Janet Scudder (1869–1940) of Terre Haute was one of the most successful female sculptors of the early 1900s. She created many of the fountains in Paris, France, and throughout the United States. Her sculptures are shown in many museums, including the Metropolitan Museum of Art in New York City and the Huntington Library near Pasadena, California. Two of her most famous fountains—Frog Fountain and Tortoise Boy—are in Indiana museums.

In the early 1900s, a group of five Indiana painters displayed their art at a Chicago exhibit. Known as the Hoosier Group, these artists—T.C. Steele, Johns Ottis Williams, William Forsythe, Otto Stark, and Richard Gruelle—had decided to reflect Indiana's beauty in their works. They dreamed of developing a Hoosier style of art and sharing it with the world. At the 1904 World's Fair in St. Louis, they received a unique honor—their own building to display their art.

Indiana's Food

Hoosiers' favorite foods are as varied as Hoosiers themselves. They enjoy traditional fare made with recipes handed down by family members, as well as contemporary cooking.

TRADITIONAL AMISH SPECIALTIES

The Amish, a Protestant religious group, settled in Indiana in 1841. Their plentiful meals reflect both their European and midwestern heritage. Typical dishes include sausages, bacon, sauerkraut, chicken corn soup, breads, and jellies. Desserts, too, are rich and hearty. Fruit pies and shoofly pie, a sweet cake-like pie, are Amish favorites.

An Amish woman carries a tray of some of the group's homemade treats.

Indiana Butterscotch Pie

An easy-to-make Hoosier favorite. **Have an adult help you.**

Pie ingredients:

1 & ½ cup brown sugar

4 tablespoons butter

⅓ cup flour

½ teaspoon salt

2 egg yolks

2 cups milk

1 baked pie shell

Meringue ingredients:

2 egg whites

pinch salt

2 tablespoons
confectioners' sugar

dash vanilla

Preheat oven to 400°F. Melt brown sugar and butter in saucepan. Add rest of ingredients. Cook until thick in double boiler. Pour into baked crust. To make the meringue, beat all ingredients together in a chilled metal bowl with a mixer until hard peaks form. Top pie with meringue. Bake until meringue turns a light golden brown.

Indiana's Folklore and Legends

Legends and folklore are stories that are not totally true but are often based on bits of truth. These stories helped people understand things that could not be easily explained. They also taught lessons to younger generations. All peoples have passed down stories as part of their culture.

THE LEGEND OF JOHNNY APPLESEED

Known as John Chapman in real life, Johnny Appleseed was born in Massachusetts in 1774. In the early 1800s he moved to the lands of the Northwest Territory, which included present-day Indiana. Appleseed grew and sold trees and plants for a living. He began taking sacks of apple seeds into the wilderness, planting rows of trees along the way, surrounding his orchards with brush fences to keep out animals. He traveled by himself and lived with the Native Americans.

According to legend, Appleseed became sick and died in 1845 near present-day Fort Wayne.

He roamed the wilderness for about 50 years, planting untold millions of apple trees. When settlers finally began moving into the area, they found Appleseed's trees bearing fruit. The seeds from these trees may well have been carried west of the Mississippi River.

DEVIL'S BONES IN INDIANA

Rochester's Lake Manitou, in north-central Indiana, is sometimes called Devil's Lake. The local Native Americans once knew it as Lake of the Water Spirit's Bones. *Manitou* means "powerful nature spirit," but it was translated as "devil" or "demon" in English.

Native Americans told of giant water creatures lurking at the bottom of the lake. As proof, they pointed to the huge stone bones that appeared from time to time along the lakeshore. The bones showed how big and fearsome these monsters were. Because of the monsters, the Native Americans avoided fishing or camping at the lake.

When settlers from states in the east moved to Indiana, they not only heard the eerie stories but, beginning in 1828, reported seeing the monsters in the lake as well as the bones along the shore. They, too, avoided the lake.

Mastodons stood eight to ten feet tall and weighed four to six tons.

The source of the story may stem from the **fossilized** bones of mastodons that are sometimes found sticking out of the lakeshore. Mastodons resembled huge, hairy elephants. They lived in North America at the time of the glaciers, and their bones are still buried in northern Indiana. As the soil wears away, these bones often become visible on the lakeshores and stream banks. These bones may have inspired the Native American legend.

Indiana's Sports Teams

Many Hoosiers are huge sports fans. They cheer for baseball, football, soccer, and many other sports teams. Their favorite sport is basketball—professional basketball, college basketball, and high school basketball.

PROFESSIONAL SPORTS

The Indianapolis Colts kick off home football games in the RCA Dome. The Colts moved to Indianapolis in 1984. In 1995 the team nearly made it to the Super Bowl, losing 20-16 to the Pittsburgh Steelers in the conference title game.

The Indiana Pacers of the NBA came to Indianapolis in 1987. They were named the "Pacers" in part because of the state's history with harness racing pacers as well as with the pace cars that lead the Indy 500. The Pacers were often playoff contenders in the 1990s, and they made the NBA finals in 2000.

When the Indianapolis Colts's season tickets went on sale in April 1984, the Hoosier response was overwhelming—143,000 requests in two weeks.

Reggie Miller, Pacers Superstar

Drafted in 1987, Reggie Miller quickly soared to become the Pacers's star player. In 1990 Miller was chosen to play his first all-star game. In 1993 he became the Pacers's all-time leading scorer. In the 1990s Miller won many play-off games with last-second heroics.

Perhaps what is most surprising about Miller's career is that he ever became a professional athlete. He was born with a hip deformity and wore leg braces for the first four years of his life. Doctors questioned whether he would ever be able to walk without help. Nevertheless, after the braces came off, Miller worked hard and became one of the NBA's best players.

COLLEGE SPORTS

Indiana's colleges and universities all field a wide variety sports teams. The Indiana University Hoosiers played their first-ever basketball game back in 1901 and has secured a place in basketball history. The team has won five men's basketball national championships. The Purdue Boilermakers, in West Lafayette, won their first women's basketball national championship in 1999.

The University of Notre Dame played its first football game in 1887. Through the years, the team would win eleven national championships and produce seven **Heisman Trophy** winners. No one knows for sure where the team's nickname, "The Fighting Irish," came from. It may date back to a game with Northwestern University in 1899. According to a 1929 Notre Dame newspaper, the nickname was originally used to describe the team during its early—and losing—days. Today, the nickname is used proudly!

Indiana University's Hoosiers are a statewide favorite.

On October 18, 1924, Knute Rockne's Fighting Irish led Notre Dame to victory over the Army, 13-7. The four key players became known as the Four Horsemen. They posed for this photograph after their Army win.

THE MILAN HIGH SCHOOL MIRACLE

Back in 1954, tiny Milan High School (162 students) beat Muncie Central (1,662 students) in the Indiana boys state high school basketball championship. With three seconds left to play and a tied score, Milan's Bobby Plump took a one-hand shot from fifteen feet out and won the game. The Milan team became legends! The 1986 movie *Hoosiers* was based on Milan's victory.

Crispus Attucks High School

Another Hoosier basketball legend was taking shape in the 1950s. African American students at Indianapolis's Crispus Attucks High School overcame poverty and racial barriers to achieve fame. Led by talented players, including Oscar Robertson, the Crispus Attucks Tigers won the state championship two years in a row. In 1955 Attucks became the first all-black school to win a championship, and in 1956, it became the first undefeated state champion. Oscar Robertson went on to become a superstar with the Milwaukee Bucks.

Indiana's Businesses and Products

The Hoosier State boasts a diverse economy. Agriculture is the leading business, but steel making, manufacturing, and health care are important to the state as well.

FARM PRODUCTS

Indiana is a leading farm state, with about 64,000 farms, averaging about 254 acres each. Farms cover almost 15.5 million acres of land—70 percent of the state. Indiana's leading crop is corn. It ranks fourth in the nation in corn production. The Hoosier State ranks in the top ten for many other farm products, including soybeans, eggs, mint, hogs, tomatoes, and turkeys.

Indiana produces sweet corn as well as corn for popcorn and animal feed.

One hundred years ago, farmers used horse-drawn plows to till their fields. Most farm work was done by hand. Today, modern equipment and up-to-date farming methods keep Indiana an agricultural leader. Even computers help farms be more productive. Indiana exports more than $5 billion in farm goods each year. The state's five leading

Orville Redenbacher Popcorn

Orville Redenbacher, a Hoosier, attended Purdue University and studied farming. He **crossbred** different types of corn before developing his famous popping corn. Redenbacher himself came up with the name "Gourmet Popcorn," but an ad agency suggested placing Redenbacher's name and face on the package. Redenbacher sold his business in 1976 for several million dollars. Valparaiso was home to Redenbacher's first popcorn factory. The city, known as "The Popcorn Capital of the World," honors Redenbacher and popcorn with a festival and parade every September.

farm exports are soybeans, feed grains, meat, wheat, and poultry.

INDUSTRIAL PRODUCTS

Indiana is a leader in the steel industry. Steel mills in the northern part of the state continue to produce a variety of steel products, including raw steel, rails, wire, and tubes. Indiana is also a leading producer of electric equipment, transportation equipment, and chemical products.

During the **Civil War** (1861–1865), the Studebaker brothers of South Bend provided wagons for the Union army. After the war, they supplied wagons to pioneers moving west. After a few years of experimenting, the Studebakers made their first automobile in 1902. By 1917 about 350,000 Studebaker cars were on the road, making the company one of the most successful of the early automakers.

During World War II (1941–1945), the Studebakers made trucks and airplane engines. After the war, they rushed back into automobile production. During the 1950s, the company fell on hard times. The company eventually moved to Canada in 1964, taking a piece of Indiana's auto heritage with it. The last Studebaker car was made in 1966.

The Ball Corporation

Founded in 1880 by the five Ball brothers—Edmund, Frank, George, Lucius, and William— the Ball Corporation is probably most famous for making glass jars used for home canning fresh fruits and vegetables. In 1996 the Ball Corporation left the glass business to specialize in aerospace products and plastic containers.

Now based in Boulder, Colorado, its sales are about $3.5 billion a year. Although the company is no longer in Indiana, its greatest contribution to the state remains Ball State University in Muncie. In 1918 the Ball family bought the university, which had opened in 1899 as a teachers' college, and gave it to the state.

PHARMACEUTICAL PRODUCTS

Many health care industries call Indiana home. Among them is Eli Lilly, a worldwide pharmaceutical company. Eli Lilly's corporate headquarters are located in Indianapolis. The company also holds research and manufacturing centers in Clinton, Greenfield, and Lafayette. The Hoosier state is also a leading manufacturer of artificial body parts that help people after serious accidents or surgery.

MINING AND QUARRYING

Southwestern Indiana is home to rich coal mines that produce high-quality coal, which causes less pollution. The state's largest underground mine—more than 9 square miles—is King's Station Mine in Gibson County, south of Princeton. It closed in 1972. Southern Indiana is still home to large coalfields. The area also holds the state's limestone fields. Generations of "cutters" have quarried the stone for buildings across the country.

Attractions and Landmarks

About 53 million people visit Indiana each year. They spend more than $6 billion enjoying the Hoosier State's parks, lakes, historic sites, and other attractions.

LINCOLN BOYHOOD HOME

Located in Lincoln City, northeast of Evansville, is the original cabin in which Abraham Lincoln lived from age 7 to 21. The Lincolns had moved to Indiana from Kentucky in 1816. Also on the grounds is the grave of Lincoln's mother and a **living-history** farm of the times.

ANGEL MOUNDS HISTORIC SITE

Angel Mounds State Historic Site in southwestern Indiana, near Evansville, was home to people of the Middle Mississippian culture. From about C.E. 1050 to 1400, the town prospered and grew to be the largest in Indiana at the time. A **stockade** made of wattle and daub—woven sticks filled in with mud—protected the several thousand people who lived in the town from unfriendly groups in the area. In time, Angel Mounds became the center of a large

Young Abraham Lincoln learned many skills living in Indiana.

trading community. Then suddenly, around 1400, the Mississippian people deserted it. The reasons are unknown. It is one of the best-preserved prehistoric Native American sites in the United States.

McCormick's Creek State Park

The first state park in Indiana, McCormick's Creek, includes limestone formations and waterfalls. A mile-long canyon cuts down through limestone 100 feet thick. Located along the White River, visitors can hike through the thick forests or walk in the canyons.

Eugene V. Debs Home

Eugene V. Debs was the founder of the **Socialist party** in the United States. His **Victorian-style** home is located in Terre Haute. Debs was a five-time presidential candidate. His views led to many reforms, including woman **suffrage,** child-labor laws, and labor unions. Today, the house is open as a museum.

McCormick's Creek is about 14 miles northwest of Bloomington.

The Levi Coffin House

The Levi Coffin House, an eight-room brick home located in Fountain City, became a haven for thousands of enslaved people in the years before the **Civil War.** Runaways came to the Coffin's home at all hours of the night. Once safely in the house, the runaways would be fed and made comfortable until they gained enough strength to continue their journey. Levi Coffin was so successful that not a

Places to See in Indiana

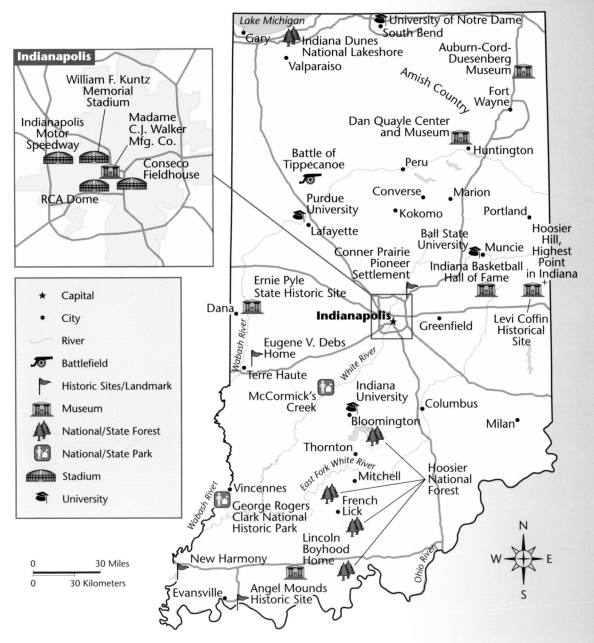

Indianapolis
- William F. Kuntz Memorial Stadium
- Madame C.J. Walker Mfg. Co.
- Indianapolis Motor Speedway
- Conseco Fieldhouse
- RCA Dome

Legend:
- ★ Capital
- • City
- ～ River
- Battlefield
- ⚐ Historic Sites/Landmark
- Museum
- National/State Forest
- National/State Park
- Stadium
- University

0   30 Miles
0   30 Kilometers

Lake Michigan
University of Notre Dame
South Bend
Gary
Indiana Dunes National Lakeshore
Valparaiso
Auburn-Cord-Duesenberg Museum
Amish Country
Fort Wayne
Dan Quayle Center and Museum
Huntington
Battle of Tippecanoe
Peru
Converse
Marion
Purdue University
Kokomo
Portland
Lafayette
Hoosier Hill, Highest Point in Indiana
Ball State University
Muncie
Conner Prairie Pioneer Settlement
Indiana Basketball Hall of Fame
Ernie Pyle State Historic Site
Levi Coffin Historical Site
Dana
Wabash River
Indianapolis
Greenfield
Eugene V. Debs Home
White River
Terre Haute
McCormick's Creek
Indiana University
Columbus
Thornton
Bloomington
Milan
East Fork White River
Mitchell
Hoosier National Forest
Wabash River
Vincennes
French Lick
George Rogers Clark National Historic Park
Lincoln Boyhood Home
New Harmony
Ohio River
Evansville
Angel Mounds Historic Site

N
W E
S

single runaway slave who stayed with him failed to reach freedom. Today, the house is listed on the National Register of Historic Places and is open as a museum.

INDIANA STATE FAIR

Indiana held its first state fair in 1852—more than 150 years ago. It was the sixth state in the country to hold a state fair. Originally, the fair was planned to encourage farming. Today at the fair, visitors can learn about water

Follow the North Star

In the years before the Civil War (1861–1865), southern Indiana hosted many important stops on the **Underground Railroad.** Through a series of safe houses, escaped slaves made their way north to Canada and freedom.

The Conner Prairie Pioneer Settlement recreates for its visitors the terrifying experience of runaway slaves. Called Follow the North Star, because runaways used the North Star to guide them, the program allows visitors to "escape" from a master. They must use their wits as they flee for about two miles, meeting both helpful and not-so-helpful people.

Thousands of visitors attend the Indiana state fair every August.

conservation, the birth of dairy cows, or corn production.

INDIANA BLACK EXPO

The Indiana Black Expo (IBE), founded in 1970, brings more than 300,000 visitors to Indianapolis every July. Religious and civic leaders wanted to showcase the arts, culture, history, and other achievements of the African American community. Today, the IBE is the largest celebration of its kind in the United States.

MADAM C.J. WALKER MANUFACTURING COMPANY

Established in Indianapolis in the early 1900s, the Madam C.J. Walker Manufacturing Company was the headquarters of one of the most successful African American–owned businesses of the time. Madam C.J.

Walker, the daughter of formerly enslaved parents, had invented a line of women's hair-care products. Her saleswomen, known as "Walker Agents," sold the products door-to-door throughout the United States.

The Madam C.J. Walker Manufacturing Company housed a beauty school, a laboratory, and a factory that employed about 3,000 people. Today, the Madam C.J. Walker Theater Center occupies the building. A cultural center and museum, open to the public, are also located in the old factory.

Madam C.J. Walker became one of the most successful entrepreneurs in the United States.

THE AUBURN-CORD-DUESENBERG MUSEUM

Located in Auburn in northeastern Indiana, the Auburn-Cord-Duesenberg Museum reflects the long-standing automotive heritage of Indiana. At least 21 different types of cars were made in Indiana. Among these were the Auburn and the Cord, two models that were popular in the 1920s and 1930s. The sleek Duesenberg was one of the most expensive cars made in the United States. The saying "It's a Duesy!" comes from the fact that Duesenbergs were special cars. The museum also holds such rare cars as John Lennon's 1956 Bentley and a 1948 Tucker—one of only 51 made.

About 140 unique and rare cars are displayed at the Auburn-Cord-Duesenburg Museum.

Notre Dame's golden dome is perhaps one of the most recognized college landmarks in the country.

THE UNIVERSITY OF NOTRE DAME

Founded in 1842, the University of Notre Dame in South Bend quickly grew into one of the largest Catholic universities in the world. In 1869 the university started the nation's first Catholic law school and in 1873 the first Catholic college of engineering.

Today, a golden dome topped with a statue of Mary, the mother of Jesus, or Our Lady (Notre Dame), rises above the campus. The statue was a gift from nearby Saint Mary's College. It is sixteen feet tall and weighs more than two tons. Both the statue and the dome are covered in 23-karat gold leaf.

THE INDIANA DUNES

Mount Baldy at Lake Michigan is the largest "living" dune in the United States. Water, wind, and waves are moving this 135-foot dune south from the lake at four or five feet a year.

Indiana Dunes National Lakeshore is located about 50 miles southeast of Chicago in northwest Indiana. The national lakeshore runs for nearly 25 miles along southern Lake Michigan. The Indiana Dunes are home to about 1,400 different types of plants, about 90 of which are **endangered.** The Indiana Dunes were made part of the National Park Service in 1966.

Map of Indiana

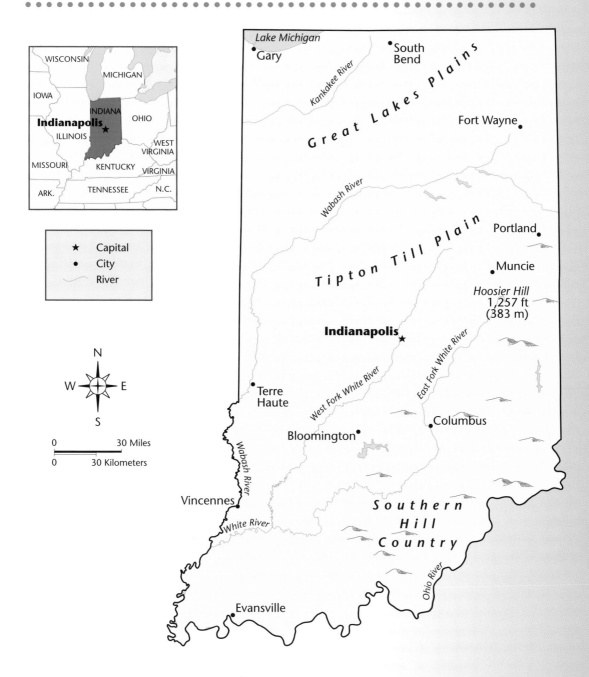

WISCONSIN

MICHIGAN

IOWA

INDIANA

ILLINOIS

OHIO

Indianapolis ★

WEST VIRGINIA

MISSOURI

KENTUCKY

VIRGINIA

ARK.

TENNESSEE

N.C.

★ Capital
• City
〜 River

N
W   E
S

0   30 Miles
0   30 Kilometers

Lake Michigan

• Gary

• South Bend

Kankakee River

G r e a t   L a k e s   P l a i n s

Fort Wayne •

Wabash River

T i p t o n   T i l l   P l a i n

Portland •

• Muncie

Hoosier Hill
1,257 ft
(383 m)

Indianapolis ★

West Fork White River

East Fork White River

• Terre Haute

• Columbus

Bloomington •

Wabash River

Vincennes •

White River

**S o u t h e r n
H i l l
C o u n t r y**

Ohio River

Evansville •

Glossary

alloy a mixture of two or more metals that usually results in a stronger metal

appeals case a court case that the defendant asks a higher court to review

appellate court a court that hears cases from a lower court

artifact an object or tool made by humans

cede to give up control or possession of such things as land or trading rights, often as a result of a treaty

centennial the one-hundredth anniversary of an event

Civil War (1861–1865) in the U.S., the war between the North and the South

crossbred the mixing of two different varieties of a plant or animal

delegate individuals elected to represent the people (as a convention or meeting)

diesel a type of engine that burns fuel oil

endangered used to refer to a plant or animal that might become extinct or that no longer exists

enlightenment a belief in peoples' abilities and human progress

federal government the government of the United States

fossilize the turning of a once-living thing into a stone-like material, over a period of millions of years

glaciers thick, slow-moving sheets of ice

Heisman Trophy an award given to the most valuable college football player

humid-continental climate a type of climate that generally includes warm, humid summers and cold winters

jury a group of people summoned by law and sworn to hear a legal case and hand down a verdict based on evidence presented in a court of law

living-history the reenactment of past events, often at a farm, museum, or battle site

moraines low ridges made of rocks and soil left behind by glaciers

National Road the first road built entirely with federal money, it stretched from Cumberland, Maryland, to Vandalia, Illinois

New France the name for France's colonies in North America in the 1500s, 1600s, and 1700s

nomadic refers to people who move from place to place

obelisk a four-sided pillar

Republican member of one of the two main political parties in the United States today

silt rich soil that is left behind by a river or a stream

Socialist party a political party that favored government ownership of public utilities and increased worker rights

stockade a fort-like structure made of strong timber

suborbital a flight into space that does not involve traveling at least once around Earth

suffrage being able to vote

temperate climate a type of climate that has almost equally long summers and winters

tornado a violent windstorm with a funnel-shaped cloud that moves in a narrow path across the land

transistor a small device that helped conduct electrical signals, as in a radio or television, before the invention of computer chips

Underground Railroad a series of secret places where escaped slaves hid as they moved north to freedom

Victorian style a type of building style popular in the late 1800s and early 1900s, usually characterized by detailed ornamentation

More Books to Read

Boekhoff, P. M. and Stuart A. Kallen. *Indiana (Seeds of a Nation).* San Diego: Kidhaven Press, 2001.

Brunelle, Lynn and Jean Craven. *Indiana: The Hoosier State.* New York: World Almanac Education, 2002.

Butler, Dori Hillestad. *H Is for Hoosier.* Black Earth, Wisc.: Trail Books, 2001.

Cullen, Lynn. *Nelly in the Wilderness.* New York: HarperCollins Children's Books, 2002.

Heinrichs, Ann. *Indiana.* Danbury, Conn.: Children's Press, 2000.

Index

About the Author

D.J. Ross is a writer and educator with more than 25 years of experience in education. He has lived in many states and frequently has visited other areas of the country. He lives in the midwest with his three basset hounds.